WHEN A MAN DECIDES TO HEAL

A guide for men who want to grow… and women who need to understand the difference.

By Earl Butler

TABLE OF CONTENTS

COPYRIGHT

DEDICATION

AN IMPORTANT NOTE ON HEALING

A NOTE FROM EARL BUTLER

INTRODUCTION

ISBN: 979-8-9938147-4-2 (Paperback)

Published by EB Gold Publishing™
2320 Drusilla Lane, Suite A #1103
Baton Rouge, LA 70809

Publisher Information
www.ebgoldpublishing.com

Author & Updates
www.earlbutlerbooks.com
Instagram:earlbutlerbooks
Printed in the United States of America

A Reflection

Hurt people hurt people. It's a sickness that spreads through the body, breaking you down at every level. You become toxic. Negative. Selfish. I was broken for many years, so I understand where people are. Fear of vulnerability. Unhealed wounds. Bitterness. Frustration. I'm not speaking from theory. I'm speaking from experience, and Love always prevails ❧ — Earl Butler

DEDICATION

To every man who grew up without the language for his pain… and every woman who tried to love him through storms she didn't create. This book is for the ones who are ready to break the cycle, and for the ones who need to understand why healing matters.

AN IMPORTANT NOTE ON HEALING

This book is not written as medical advice, psychological treatment, or professional counseling. I am not a licensed therapist, counselor, or mental health professional. I believe deeply in therapy. I believe in counseling. I believe in professional support. But I also believe in honesty about access. At different points in my life, the help I needed wasn't available. Sometimes it wasn't affordable. Sometimes it wasn't accessible. Sometimes I didn't even have the language to ask for it. This book exists for those moments. It is written from lived experience, reflection, and personal growth—not from a clinical perspective. It is meant to offer awareness, clarity, and emotional understanding—not diagnosis or treatment. If you are dealing with severe emotional distress, trauma, depression, or thoughts of harming yourself or others, professional help is not optional—it is necessary. And seeking that help is a sign of strength, not weakness. This book does not replace therapy. It does not compete with counseling. It does not claim to heal you on its own.

What it does is start conversations many men were never taught how to have—and help women understand what healing actually looks like when it's real. Use this book as a mirror. Use it as a guide. Use it as a beginning. And when you can, pair it with professional support that helps you go even deeper. Healing is not a destination. It's a process. And no man is meant to walk it alone.

— Earl Butler

A NOTE FROM EARL BUTLER

I didn't write this book to point fingers or assign blame. I wrote it to bring clarity. This book is for men who are willing to look inward, and for women who want to better understand what that inward work looks like. Healing is not about perfection, and it is not about rewriting the past. It is about honesty, accountability, and growth.

Some chapters may feel uncomfortable. That's intentional. Growth often begins where comfort ends. My book is not meant to diagnose, judge, or instruct you how to live. I'm offering an invitation to reflect, to recognize patterns, and to choose better from this point forward.

If even one page causes you to pause and see yourself more clearly, then this book has done its job.

INTRODUCTION

"When a man refuses to heal, the people closest to him pay the price." I didn't understand that truth until later in my life. Not because I didn't care… but because no one ever taught me how deep unhealed pain runs through a man. As men, we learn early how to survive. We learn how to keep moving. We learn how to act like we're fine, even when everything inside is falling apart. We learn silence. We learn toughness. We learn how to put our wounds in our back pocket and pretend they don't hurt. But here's the part nobody talks about. Those wounds don't stay hidden. They show up in how we love.

They show up in how we talk. They show up in what we run from, what we fight for, and what we destroy without meaning to. The people who feel it the most are the ones who love us the hardest. Women feel it first. Children feel it next. Family feels it last. A broken man can love deeply—but he will still hurt people unintentionally, not because he wants to…but because pain always leaks where healing never happened. And if you're reading this—you've probably lived on one side of that truth.

Maybe you're a woman who tried to love a man through wounds he never confronted. Maybe you're a man who sees himself in that silence. Maybe you're someone trying to break a cycle that's been following your family for generations.

Or maybe you're simply tired of surviving emotions you never had the chance to understand. Whatever brought you here, this book is not written to shame you, blame you, or break you down. It's written to clarify what's been confusing you. It's written to name what you couldn't explain. It's written to guide you toward a better version of yourself—whether you're the man doing the healing or the woman trying to understand it.

Because the truth is simple. Healing isn't just about the man. It's about everyone connected to him. So if you're ready to learn the difference between a man who wants to grow and a man who's actually doing the work…If you're ready to understand the emotional blueprint behind a man's behavior…If you're ready to recognize the signs—both the red flags and the green ones…Then you're exactly where you need to be. And from this point forward, I'm going to talk to you the same way I wish someone talked to me years ago—with honesty, clarity, and respect.

CHAPTER 1

THE PAIN HE NEVER TALKS ABOUT

Most men don't wake up choosing to be distant. They don't wake up choosing to shut down, push away, or love from a distance. It's not intentional. It's inherited. Every man has a story behind the way he loves, even if he never says a word about it. And here's the part most people never understand. A man's silence isn't the absence of emotion. It's the overflow of it. Men grow up being taught to hide what hurts. To stay strong. To keep moving. To hold everything inside because "talking about it" was never a safe option.

So he grows up with a heart that learned how to survive, but never learned how to heal. And what he doesn't talk about becomes the very thing that shapes how he treats the people who love him. When a man pulls away, there's a story behind that. When he doesn't know how to communicate, there's a story behind that. When he shuts down instead of opening up, there's a story behind that. When he gets angry fast or avoids conflict completely, there's a story behind that. You're not dealing with a reaction. You're dealing with the survival habits he built as a boy.

Habits he never unlearned. Patterns he never examined. Pain he never processed. Questions he never felt safe asking. Emotions he was never taught how to understand. He isn't emotionless. He's overwhelmed. He isn't cold. He's guarded. He isn't uncaring. He's unhealed. And women often take this personally, not because they're wrong, but because they feel everything he doesn't know how to say. A woman might think. "He's distant because of me."

"He doesn't communicate because he doesn't love me." "He's shutting down because he's done with the relationship." But most of the time, it's none of those things. He's not shutting down on you. He's shutting down because he never learned how to stay open. And the truth that hurts the most—the truth women feel deep in their chest—is this. She becomes the emotional punching bag for battles he started fighting long before he met her. Not because he wants to hurt her…but because he never healed the boy who still lives inside him.

The signs are subtle at first. He's present, but not connected. He listens, but doesn't respond emotionally. He cares, but doesn't know how to show it. He loves, but doesn't know how to express it. He gets overwhelmed by normal conversations. He shuts down when things get too real. He disappears emotionally when he feels pressure. And the hardest truth of all, he loves her from a place he hasn't healed from.

Which means the love has limits, not because he wants it that way, but because his unhealed pain built those limits for him. A man will never tell you he's scared of being vulnerable. He won't say he's afraid you'll see the broken parts of him. He won't admit he doesn't want to disappoint you. He won't confess that he doesn't know how to be the man you need yet. He won't explain that he never learned how to handle emotions the right way. Most of the time, he doesn't even understand himself fully.

Instead, he goes quiet. He retreats. He gets defensive. He changes the subject. He buries himself in work. He avoids emotional moments. He pretends he's fine when he's anything but. That silence isn't strength. It's fear dressed up as strength. Healing isn't natural for most men. Not because they're incapable, but because they were never taught how. Most men grow up without emotional language. Without emotional safety. Without emotional examples. Without emotional support. Without emotional understanding. And without those things, healing feels like failure.

Talking feels like a weakness. Being vulnerable feels like exposure. Admitting pain feels like defeat. So he hides what hurts, not realizing that hiding it is the very thing that keeps him stuck. Every man has a story he never told. A heartbreak he never healed. A moment that changed him. A silence he never learned to break. A boy inside him who still feels abandoned, embarrassed, rejected, or misunderstood.

And until he faces that pain, until he decides to heal, he will keep spilling emotional pain into every relationship he enters, even the good ones. Women can't fix it. Love can't fix it. A new partner can't fix it. Time can't fix it. Healing is a decision. A personal one. A necessary one. A powerful one. And when a man finally chooses that path…everything changes.

CHAPTER 2

WHAT AN UNHEALED MAN LOOKS LIKE IN A RELATIONSHIP

People think pain always shows up loudly. But the truth is…it often walks in quietly. An unhealed man doesn't always look broken from the outside. Sometimes he looks calm. Sometimes he looks confident. Sometimes he looks like he has everything together. But inside, he's fighting battles he never talks about. And those battles show up in the way he loves. Not because he intends to hurt anyone, but because he's still fighting battles inside himself. The signs aren't always dramatic. In fact, they're often subtle. Slow. Silent.

Easy to overlook until it's too late. Women feel these signs first, long before he ever says a word. He gives effort, but not consistency. He gives affection, but not emotional presence. He gives conversation, but not vulnerability. He gives connection, but not commitment. He gives attention, but not clarity. He doesn't mean to be halfway. He doesn't mean to be confusing. He doesn't mean to be unpredictable. He's just unhealed. And unhealed men love in pieces. One minute he's warm. The next he's cold. One day he's open. The next he shuts down.

One moment he's expressive. An hour later he's silent. Not because he's playing games. But because his emotions don't have a stable foundation. They're built on top of old pain. An unhealed man doesn't know how to sit still with his own feelings. So he won't know how to sit still with yours. He gets defensive fast because defensiveness is easier than honesty. He feels attacked even when you're trying to help him. He takes things personally that weren't meant to hurt him. He hears criticism where you meant compassion.

He hears pressure where you meant partnership. He hears danger where you meant love. That's what unhealed trauma does. It distorts messages. It twists meanings. It turns comfort into confusion and turns safety into fear. A woman might try harder. Speak softer. Give more. Give space. Explain. Re-explain. Pray for him. Pour into him. Hold everything together. But an unhealed man isn't someone you can out-love. Love can reach him, but it can't change him. Only healing can do that. You'll know you're dealing with an unhealed man when he avoids responsibility.

He'll acknowledge the problem, but not fix it. He'll apologize, but not improve. He'll promise, but not produce. He doesn't do this out of disrespect. He does it because he's emotionally overwhelmed. He doesn't have the tools yet. He doesn't have the emotional capacity yet. He doesn't have the internal structure to handle the weight of healthy love. When things start to feel real, he pulls back.

Not because he doesn't care, but because emotional depth feels unfamiliar. He avoids conversations that ask him to go deeper than he knows how. He stays present on the surface, while quietly retreating underneath. He wants connection—but without the weight of accountability that comes with being fully seen. An unhealed man might look strong, but not in the ways that matter. His strength is survival strength, not emotional strength. Survival strength helps you carry pain.

Emotional strength helps you stop carrying it. Survival strength helps you block out the world. Emotional strength helps you let love in. Survival strength helps you keep moving. Emotional strength helps you grow. A man who hasn't healed yet is stuck in survival mode. He's reacting to life instead of responding to it. He's protecting himself from feelings instead of learning from them. He's avoiding love instead of accepting it. And the saddest part? He wants to love deeply. He just doesn't trust himself enough to try. Women often stay because they see his potential.

They see the man he could become. They see the softness beneath the hurt. They see the loyalty in his intentions. They see the good in his heart. But potential isn't the same as readiness. And potential without healing becomes pain. Because an unhealed man won't stop loving you…but he will stop being able to love you well. And it's not your job to fix him.

Love can support healing, but it cannot replace it. No woman deserves to carry the emotional burden of a man who refuses to face himself. No woman deserves to feel like she's not enough when the real battle is inside him. No woman deserves to confuse chaos with passion, or distance with uncertainty, or inconsistency with "maybe he just needs time." Healing isn't about time. Healing is about choice. And until he makes that choice…he isn't ready for a healthy relationship. Not because he doesn't care about you, but because he doesn't know how to care for himself.

The next chapter explains what happens when a man finally makes that choice—when he decides to truly heal, from the inside out. And that's when everything changes.

CHAPTER 3

WHY POTENTIAL ISN'T READINESS

A lot of relationships fall apart because of one simple belief. "He has potential." Potential is powerful. It's hopeful. It's inspiring. It makes you believe in what a person could be. But here's the truth most people learn the hard way. Potential is not the same as readiness. Potential is what a man can become. Readiness is who he chooses to be right now. A man's potential will show you his heart. But his readiness will show you his habits. And no matter how good a man's intentions are, no matter how deeply he cares, no matter how promising his spirit is…If he isn't healed, he isn't ready. Women often confuse the two because potential is loud. It's bright.

It's attractive. It's soft around the edges. It speaks to what could be. It paints a picture of a future he might not be prepared to build. Readiness is quiet. It shows up in consistency. It shows up in accountability. It shows up in emotional responsibility. It shows up in choices, not promises. Potential makes you feel. Readiness makes you see. An unhealed man can have incredible potential. He can be kind. He can be loyal in his spirit. He can be supportive on his good days. He can be loving in the moments he feels safe. He can show glimpses of the man he wants to become. But glimpses are not growth.

And moments are not maturity. A man who is not ready will give you pieces of himself, but never the whole. He will be intentional today, and absent tomorrow. Warm one moment, cold the next. Not because he wants to fail you, but because he's still failing himself. Potential is the dream. Readiness is the reality of him. There is a difference between a man who means well and a man who lives well. Between a man who sees the problem and a man who works on it.

Between a man who apologizes and a man who changes. A man with potential will tell you what he hopes to be. A man who is ready will show you what he's becoming. You'll feel this difference in your spirit long before your mind admits it. Potential will make you wait. Readiness will make you grow. Potential will keep you hoping. Readiness will give you peace. Potential will pull you in emotionally. Readiness will meet you emotionally. Women often hold on because they see the future version of him. But healing doesn't happen in the future. Healing only happens in the present.

A man cannot love you from his potential. He can only love you from his readiness. And if he still hasn't healed, if he hasn't confronted his patterns, if he hasn't looked at the pain that shapes him…He is not ready. He may want to be. He may try to be. He may promise to be.

But wanting, trying, and promising are not the same as preparing. Readiness requires work. Real work. Internal work. Honest work. Uncomfortable work. It requires a man to admit to himself what he spent years avoiding. It requires him to apologize to the parts of himself he abandoned. It requires him to understand how his past shaped his behavior.

It requires him to take responsibility for his emotional patterns. And until he does that, his potential will always outweigh his reality. No woman can fill that gap for him. No relationship can complete that journey for him. No amount of love can replace that work. A man can only meet you where he has met himself. If he hasn't faced himself yet, he cannot fully face you. Potential is a promise. Readiness is proof. And a healed man knows the difference.

CHAPTER 4

THE MOMENT A MAN DECIDES TO HEAL

Every man has a moment where life stops him. Not physically. Not loudly. But internally. A quiet moment where he can no longer outrun the version of himself he's been avoiding. Healing doesn't begin when a man is in crisis. Healing begins when a man finally realizes that the way he has been living is costing him more than the pain he's been avoiding. There is always a turning point. It might come from heartbreak. It might come from losing someone he cared about.

It might come from hurting someone he never intended to hurt. It might come from finally seeing himself clearly for the first time. Or it may come from simply being tired of carrying the same weight every day. But that moment itself is unmistakable. It's the moment he understands that his survival habits are no longer protecting him—they're limiting him. It's the moment he realizes that shutting down isn't strength, and silence isn't control.

It's the moment he sees his emotional patterns not as reactions, but as wounds. A man decides to heal when he recognizes that the people who love him are experiencing pain he never meant to give. And that realization hits deeper than anything else. It's not guilt. It's awareness. It's suddenly knowing that the hurt he carries has been spilling into his relationships, his conversations, his decisions, his reactions and his silence. For the first time, he looks inward instead of pointing outward.

He starts asking himself the questions he avoided. He starts acknowledging the feelings he buried. He starts admitting the truths he ran from. This moment isn't loud. It's honest. And honesty is something most unhealed men haven't allowed themselves to feel. A man who is ready to heal stops protecting his wounds and starts confronting them. He stops blaming life for what shaped him and starts taking responsibility for what he became. He stops expecting others to tolerate his patterns and starts learning how to break them.

Healing begins the moment he decides he is done repeating the same history. And women feel this shift instantly. Not because he becomes perfect overnight, but because he becomes present. More aware. More accountable. More open. More willing. A man who has decided to heal listens differently. He speaks differently. He apologizes differently. He loves differently. He handles conflict differently. He shows up differently.

He feels differently. Healing doesn't make him emotional. It makes him honest. Healing doesn't make him weak. It makes him aware. Healing doesn't make him soft. It makes him strong in ways he's never been strong before. The moment a man decides to heal is the moment he stops living as a reaction to the boy he used to be. He steps into responsibility. He steps into alignment. He steps into purpose. He steps into maturity. He steps into the version of himself that stopped surviving and started growing.

He becomes a man who can love without fear, communicate without shutting down, and lead without controlling. Because healing isn't about being perfect. It's about being present. Being honest. Being aware. Being accountable. Being willing. Being better than yesterday. The moment a man chooses to heal is the moment his entire life begins to shift—from the inside out. And that's when the man he can be finally starts to become the man he is becoming.

CHAPTER 5

WHAT HEALING LOOKS LIKE IN A MAN

Healing doesn't happen all at once. It happens quietly. It happens gradually. It happens internally long before anyone else can see it. A man who begins to heal doesn't announce it. He reveals it through the way he starts showing up in life. You'll notice it in his awareness. He begins paying attention to the things he used to ignore. He listens without being defensive. He pauses before reacting. He becomes conscious of his patterns instead of being controlled by them. You'll notice it in his presence. He doesn't disappear when things get uncomfortable.

He doesn't shut down when emotions rise. He stays engaged in conversations that require honesty. Healing gives him the courage to stay instead of escape. You'll notice it in his responsibility. He begins acknowledging the impact of his behavior. He stops blaming the world for what he created. He stops blaming his past for what he's choosing in the present. He no longer hides behind excuses or explanations. Healing makes him accountable.

You'll notice it in how he communicates and handles conflict. He expresses himself with intention instead of impulse. He chooses clarity over confusion. He listens to understand, not to defend. He faces problems directly instead of avoiding them or punishing others with silence. Healing teaches him emotional discipline. You'll notice it in his emotional maturity. He no longer confuses anger with strength. He no longer mistakes shutting down for control. He no longer sees vulnerability as weakness. He becomes more comfortable feeling his emotions instead of being ruled by them. Healing makes him emotionally steady.

You'll notice it in his consistency. He follows through. He keeps his word. He honors his commitments. He shows up even when it's difficult. He becomes reliable over time, not just convincing in the moment. Healing makes him dependable. You'll notice it in his relationships. He becomes safer to love. He becomes softer without becoming weak. Clearer without becoming harsh. More open without becoming unstable.

He stops loving from fear and begins loving from understanding. Healing makes him capable of intimacy. You'll notice it in the way he sees himself. He stops running from his reflection. He accepts his flaws without letting them define him. He forgives himself for the things he didn't know.

He apologizes to the version of himself who was doing the best he could with what he had. Healing gives him compassion toward himself. You'll notice it in the way he protects peace. He removes himself from chaos. He refuses to let trauma rule his life. He chooses healthier environments, healthier relationships, and healthier ways of thinking. Healing changes his environment. You'll notice it in the way he treats those he loves. He becomes gentle where he used to be guarded.

Patient where he used to be reactive. Understanding where he used to be defensive. Loving where he used to be distant. Healing makes him emotionally safe. You'll notice it in the man he becomes. Not perfect. Not flawless. Not finished. But present. Attentive. Aware. Growing. Healing doesn't turn him into someone new. It returns him to who he truly is beneath the trauma…beneath the fear…beneath the silence…beneath the old habits… beneath the history he never asked for.

 A healed man is not a different man. He's a man who is finally free. And that freedom changes everything —the way he thinks, the way he loves, the way he leads, the way he shows up for himself, and the way he shows up for others.

CHAPTER 6

LOVING A MAN WHO IS STILL HEALING

Loving a man who is healing is different from loving a man who is unhealed. He isn't running like he used to. He isn't shutting down the same way. He isn't pretending he's fine when he's clearly overwhelmed. But he's also not fully steady yet. He's learning himself. He's unlearning patterns. He's confronting emotions he used to avoid. He's trying to become a better man while still wrestling with the old version of himself. And that journey can be beautiful—but it can also be challenging. Because a healing man isn't finished. He's transitioning.

He's caught between who he was and who he's becoming. He wants to love better, but he doesn't always know how. He wants to communicate more, but sometimes slips back into silence. He wants to be consistent, but he's still learning how to carry emotional weight he once avoided. A healing man is willing—but willingness doesn't erase the process.

Women often expect healing to be a straight line. It isn't. It has progress and pauses. Breakthroughs and setbacks. Moments of clarity and moments of confusion.

But here is the difference that matters. An unhealed man avoids. A healing man tries. An unhealed man shuts down. A healing man stays present, even when uncomfortable. An unhealed man repeats patterns. A healing man recognizes them and works to change them. An unhealed man blames. A healing man takes responsibility. A healing man won't be perfect, but you will see effort. You will feel the intention.

You will notice change—not instantly, but consistently. Loving a healing man requires understanding, not saviorhood. He doesn't need you to fix him. He doesn't need you to rebuild him. He doesn't need you to become his emotional shield. He needs patience while he builds emotional muscles he never had. He needs clarity when old habits try to return. He needs space to grow without being punished for his past. He needs partnership, not pressure.

 A healing man will still have moments where he goes quiet. Moments where emotions feel heavy. Moments where he needs time to process. Moments where fear of disappointing you resurfaces. The difference now is that he communicates those moments instead of disappearing inside them. Healing teaches a man how to feel without shutting down, how to speak without fear, and how to stay without running. This is where your role becomes important—Not to do the healing for him, but to understand what healing requires.

A man who is healing needs support, but he also needs accountability. Not the kind that criticizes, but the kind that reminds him who he's becoming. He needs compassion, but not the kind that enables avoidance. He needs patience, but not the kind that tolerates repeated harm. Loving a healing man means recognizing the difference between a man who is genuinely growing and a man who is using the language of "healing" to escape responsibility. Because real healing shows up in behavior.

In communication. In consistency. In effort— both toward the relationship and toward himself. A healing man will not make you feel like you're fighting alone. He will walk with you, even if some days he walks slowly. He wants to meet you where you are, even if he's still learning how to get there. Healing is not a burden to carry together. It is a journey he must lead within himself while allowing love to make the path gentler.

The truth is simple. A man who is healing is in motion. A man who is healing is aware. A man who is healing is trying. A man who is healing is becoming. And loving that kind of man can be one of the most rewarding experiences…because you're not loving his potential—you're loving his progress. Progress is real. Progress is visible. Progress is trustworthy.

CHAPTER 7

HOW A HEALED MAN LOVES

A healed man loves differently. Not because he's perfect, not because he never gets upset, not because he no longer feels fear…but because he finally understands himself. Healing gives a man the emotional strength to love from a place that isn't wounded. It gives him clarity without confusion, maturity without chaos, and confidence without running. A healed man doesn't use love to fill emptiness. He brings love from fullness. He doesn't seek validation. He brings value.

He doesn't chase attention. He offers presence. He doesn't hide his emotions. He expresses them with intention. He doesn't fear vulnerability. He uses it to build connections. A healed man knows that loving deeply doesn't make him weak—it makes him whole. A healed man communicates. Not just when it's easy, but especially when it's uncomfortable. He speaks with honesty, listens with patience, and responds with care. He doesn't shut down. He doesn't disappear. He doesn't leave you guessing.

He lets you in, fully. A healed man is emotionally present. He pays attention to your tone,your comfort, your needs, your silence. He doesn't wait for breakdowns to show up.

He shows up daily. Not through grand gestures, but through steady consistency. A healed man is patient. He understands growth takes time. He respects that you have your own wounds, your own history, your own sensitivities. He doesn't weaponize your past or shame your emotions. He learns them. He honors them. He handles them with care. A healed man loves with clarity. You don't question where you stand. You don't decode mixed signals. You don't search for meaning in silence.

He makes his intentions known and his direction clear. A healed man leads with peace. He doesn't create chaos. He doesn't weaponize silence or pride. He resolves conflict with maturity. He apologizes without ego. He forgives without resentment. He holds himself accountable without being pushed. A healed man respects love. He treats it as something to build with—something meant to grow, something meant to last. A healed man is protective. Not possessive. Not controlling.

Not insecure. Protective. He protects your peace, your dignity, your emotional safety, and the way he chooses you—through his words, his actions, and his consistency. A healed man chooses partnership.

He considers your voice. He values your perspective. He builds with you, not around you. He understands love is a responsibility, not just a feeling. He loves with intention. With humility. With effort. With emotional intelligence. With purpose. And the most powerful difference of all. A healed man doesn't love you to heal himself. He heals himself so he can love you better. He brings stability, not confusion. Direction, not detours. Peace, not chaos. Leadership, not control. Emotional safety, not harm.

A healed man will not make you question your worth. He will confirm it. Support it. Honor it. Loving a healed man feels steady. Healthy. Intentional. Peaceful. It feels like home.

CHAPTER 8

THE NEW MAN

There comes a moment in a man's healing journey where everything settles. The noise in his mind quiets. The weight in his chest lifts. The confusion inside him clears. He steps into a version of himself he once didn't believe he could become. This is the new man. Not a perfect man. Not a flawless man. Not a man who never feels fear or pain again. But a man who is no longer ruled by the things that once controlled him. A new man walks differently. Not with arrogance, but with awareness. Not with pride, but with purpose. Not with avoidance, but with understanding. He knows what he wants, what he needs, what he refuses, and what he values.

His boundaries are healthier. His voice is stronger. His decisions are clearer. His relationships are safer. A new man honors his emotions. He doesn't hide from them. He doesn't drown in them. He doesn't fear them. He understands them. He respects them. He expresses them. A new man knows the difference between reacting and responding. Between shutting down and calming down. Between protecting himself and isolating himself. Between leaving a conversation and abandoning someone emotionally.

He becomes steady in storms because he no longer fears his own feelings. A new man treats love differently. He doesn't run from it. He doesn't sabotage it.He doesn't question whether he deserves it. He accepts it. He reciprocates it. He protects it. He grows with it. A new man treats his partner with care because he finally treats himself with care. He listens without needing to win. He apologizes without needing to defend. He communicates without shutting down. He connects without fear.

He commits without hesitation. He doesn't make love heavy. He makes love safe. A new man leads differently. Not with ego, but with clarity. Not with control, but with peace. Not with pressure, but with emotional responsibility. His presence brings calm. His mindset brings security.

His decisions bring direction. A new man doesn't fear conflict. He faces it with maturity. He resolves it with respect. He approaches it with understanding. He stops fighting the world and starts building inside it.

A new man chooses differently because he sees differently. He chooses peace over pride. Accountability over excuses. Healing over history. Consistency over chaos. Growth over comfort. Love over fear. He recognizes the boy he used to be, but he no longer lives from his wounds. He respects the man he's becoming, because he worked hard to become him. The new man is not a fantasy. He is not a myth. He is not rare. He is simply a man who allowed himself to evolve.

And the most powerful part of becoming a new man is this. He finally becomes a man who can love fully, because he finally became a man who is whole.

CHAPTER 9

WHAT I LEARNED ABOUT MYSELF

There came a point in my life where I had to face myself. Not the version I showed the world. Not the version I pretended to be. Not the version I created just to survive. But the real version of me —the one I had been avoiding for years. I learned that most of my pain didn't start as a man. It started as a boy. A boy who didn't understand why life happened the way it did. A boy who learned silence before he learned honesty. A boy who learned strength before he learned safety.

A boy who learned survival before he learned love. I learned that I carried that boy into every stage of my life. Into every relationship. Into every argument. Into every moment where I shut down instead of speaking up. Into every situation where I ran when I should've stayed. Into every place where I confused distance with peace. I realized that I wasn't cold. I was guarded. I wasn't stubborn. I was scared. I wasn't unloving. I was unhealed. And that truth hit me harder than anything life ever threw at me.

I learned that healing wasn't about blaming anyone. It wasn't about pointing fingers at my past. It wasn't about replaying everything that went wrong. It was about understanding how those moments shaped me and deciding not to let them define me.

I learned that the things I avoided were the things that needed my attention the most. The emotions I buried were the emotions I needed to understand. The patterns I dismissed were the patterns I needed to break. The habits I normalized were the habits that were quietly hurting me. I learned that my silence was loud.

People felt it. People misread it. People were affected by it. And I never realized how heavy it was because I had carried it my entire life. I learned that love doesn't run. Fear does. Love doesn't shut down. Pain does. Love doesn't push people away. History does. I learned that healing wasn't just for me. It was for everyone connected to me. My relationships. My children. My future. My family. My faith. My purpose. I learned that healing made me gentler. Not weaker. More aware. Not soft. More patient. Not passive. More grounded.

Not controlled. Healing didn't change who I was. It uncovered who I always had the potential to be. I learned that the man I wanted to become was waiting on me to stop protecting the version of me that was only built to survive. And once I let go of the old version…I finally made space for the real me. A man who can communicate. A man who can apologize. A man who can show love without fear.
A man who can lead with peace. A man who can think clearly. A man who can forgive himself. A man who can love without breaking anything in the process. A man who is whole.

I learned that healing isn't a destination. It's a decision. One I have to make every single day. And the more I learn about myself, the more I understand what I was missing all along. Clarity, peace, direction, and the emotional freedom to build the life I always deserved. This chapter isn't the end of my story. It's the introduction to the man I became before I stepped into the truth you'll read in Raised By The System. Because healing brought me here. And understanding myself is what finally freed me.

CHAPTER 10

PREPARING FOR RAISED BY THE SYSTEM

This book was never meant to give you my whole story. It was meant to prepare you for it. Because Raised By The System is not just a memoir. It's not just pages or chapters. It's the truth I lived through—and the truth I had to heal from. When I decided to write this guide, I knew it needed to come before the memoir. Not because the memoir needs explaining, but because the healing deserves understanding. Everything you read in this book—the unhealed man, the healing man, the new man—is the emotional foundation for the story that shaped me.

This book shows you the internal journey. The battles I didn't know how to name. The patterns I didn't understand. The decisions that changed my life. The growth that led me here. Raised By The System shows you the world that formed those battles. The environment. The experiences. The systems. The silence. The resilience. The reality. This book gave you the emotional lens. The memoir will give you the story. When you read my memoir, you'll understand why healing became necessary.

You'll see how those patterns were formed. You'll recognize the weight of the experiences that shaped me long before I understood myself. You'll meet the boy I was. The man I became. And the healing that bridged the two. This guide was the doorway. The memoir is the journey. Healing didn't start when I wrote my story. Healing started when I stopped running from myself. When I faced my patterns. When I accepted my truth. When I understood that becoming a better man wasn't just for me—it was for everyone connected to me.

That understanding is what allowed me to go back into my story and write it with honesty, clarity, and power. This book was the foundation. The emotional framework. The preparation. Raised By The System will take you to the beginning—and show you how far healing can take a person who refuses to stay broken. And when you finish reading it, you won't just know my story. You'll understand my heart.

CLOSING MESSAGE

Healing is not a finish line. It's a commitment. A daily choice to show up differently than you did yesterday. It's the decision to stop living from old wounds and start living from new understanding. The courage to face your past without letting it control your future. The moment you stop running and start rebuilding. If you are a man reading this, I hope you understand this truth. You are not your mistakes. You are not your patterns.

You are not the pain you grew up carrying. You are the man you decide to become. And every day you choose healing, you break generational cycles instead of repeating them. If you are a woman reading this, I hope this book gave you clarity—not confusion. Understanding—not excuses.

Discernment—not disappointment. You cannot heal a man. But you can understand him. And understanding helps you love with wisdom, not blindness. This book was written to strengthen you. To prepare you. To guide you. To protect you from mistaking potential for readiness and readiness for healing. If you've reached the end of these pages, you now understand the heart behind the journey. This wasn't the whole story. It was the foundation.

The story continues in Raised By The System. And when you read it, you will understand why healing became my greatest act of strength—and why I refuse to be the man my pain tried to turn me into. Thank you for reading. Thank you for trusting the process. Thank you for choosing healing—for yourself, for your relationships, for your family, for your future.

— Earl Butler

REFLECTIONS

When I was doing my own healing, there wasn't a guidebook for what came next...

No one told me where to start. No one told me what questions mattered. Most of the work happened quietly, when no one was watching. The pages that follow aren't instructions. They exist for honesty, not answers. Take what you need from them. Skip what doesn't speak to you. Return when you're ready. Nothing here requires completion. In the pages that follow, start writing. There's no right way to do this. One page at a time is enough.

What am I finally ready to be honest about—even if I don't
yet know what to do with it?

43

What have I been carrying that no longer belongs to who I'm becoming?

When I think about healing, what part of it have I been avoiding?

45

What patterns keep showing up in my life—even when I say I want change?

What does discipline look like for me right now—not in theory, but in real life?

What decision have I been postponing because it forces me to take responsibility?

One area of my life that needs consistent work—even when
motivation fades.

49

One habit or behavior I know I need to change—and why I've resisted it.

What boundaries would protect the progress I'm trying to make?

51

What am I consistently doing that's working, and why haven't
I acknowledged it?

Where am I still expecting results without committing to the process?

What excuse do I return to when things get uncomfortable?

54

What responsibility am I avoiding by staying distracted?

What truth have I already accepted privately but not acted on publicly?

What part of my routine needs structure instead of flexibility?

Where am I confusing rest with avoidance?

What would change if I stopped negotiating with myself?

What does follow-through look like for me right now?

What am I currently doing out of habit rather than intention?

What commitment have I made that I haven't honored?

62

What am I tolerating that's slowing my progress?

63

What does consistency require from me right now?

64

What am I asking for clarity on instead of taking action?

What part of my growth feels inconvenient, but necessary?

What does self-discipline mean for me in this season of my life?

67

What am I postponing that would bring relief if I addressed it?

What version of myself am I actively moving toward through
my daily choices?

What am I learning about myself through repetition?

What behavior keeps resurfacing when I'm under pressure?

What would change if I stopped delaying difficult
conversations?

Where am I still waiting for permission, I don't need?

What responsibility am I fully to accept now?

What part of my life needs simplification, not expansion?

What am I willing to commit to even when it feels inconvenient?

What standard am I prepared to hold myself to from here on?

What feels unresolved but ready to be addressed?

What does progress look like at this stage of my life?

What am I prepared to do differently starting now?

What am I ready to carry forward, and what am I finally willing to leave behind?

WHAT COMES NEXT

One thing that helped me was allowing myself to see forward before I knew how to get there.

These pages aren't plans.

They're space to envision a future before it's fully formed.

Write your vision and make it clear.

Then honor your written words with a check mark when they've manifested.

THE REST OF THESE PAGES ARE YOURS

www.ingramcontent.com/pod-product-compliance
Lightning Source LLC
Chambersburg PA
CBHW040124150726